NEA
SCHOOL RESTRUCTURING SERIES

Cornerstones for a New Century:

Teacher Preparation, Early Childhood Education, A National Education Index

Ernest L. Boyer

Robert M. McClure
NEA Mastery In Learning Consortium
NEA National Center for Innovation
Series Editor

nea PROFESSIONAL LIBRARY
National Education Association
Washington, D.C.

Copyright © 1992
National Education Association of the United States

Printing History
First Printing: March 1992

Note

The opinions expressed in this publication should not be construed as representing the policy or position of the National Education Association. Materials published by the NEA Professional Library are intended to be discussion documents for educators who are concerned with specialized interests of the profession.

Library of Congress Cataloging-in-Publication Data

Boyer, Ernest L.
    Cornerstones for a new century : teacher preparation, early
childhood education, a national education index / Ernest L. Boyer.
       p.   cm. — (NEA school restructuring series)
    Includes bibliographical references.
    ISBN 0-8106-1846-X
    1. Education—United States—Aims and objectives.   2. Education—
United States—Standards. 3. Education and state—United States.
4. Early childhood education—United States. 5. Teachers—Training
of—United States. I. Title. II. Series.
LA217.2.B69   1992
370'.973—dc20 91–39051
                    CIP

CONTENTS

THE AUTHOR

Ernest L. Boyer is President of the Carnegie Foundation for the Advancement of Teaching, and Senior Fellow of the Woodrow Wilson School, Princeton University. He also served as the twenty-third United States Commissioner of Education.

Dr. Boyer has had a long and distinguished career and today is often cited as one of the nation's leading educators.

FOREWORD

"All experience is an arch to build upon," wrote Henry Adams at the beginning of this century. To a school person today, that might be taken as an admonishment to attend to matters of scope and sequence and continuity in designing the curriculum. Undoubtedly, though, Adams meant considerably more than that. Likely, he'd want students to experience programs rich with ideas, history, culture, life, and language. The arch would not be built on isolated facts, far removed from the interesting humans who make up this complex world.

And that way of thinking about what our students need and deserve is at the heart of this book. Here, we get a look at the *cornerstones* of a very desirable future. This future is a place where the real needs of children and their schools are considered with an academic and moral integrity too often missing from today's discussions about improving education. In these schools the focus is on the very best we know about knowledge and children and their teachers.

The three cornerstones discussed here are built on good, substantial information about people, large and small. The first is a hard look at how teachers should be educated in the future. As has so often been the case with Ernest Boyer's work, he has talked *with* teachers about what it's like to work with today's students. He comes away with a set of propositions that, if implemented, would turn our present preparation programs directly toward serving the very people who most need help.

The second cornerstone is truly just that because here Boyer helps us to see clearly what the programs for our very youngest children must look like. The foundation that his ideal school would provide for these students would solve many of the problems now experienced by older youngsters in the upper grades.

In his final essay, Boyer provides a most rational way to think about accountability. From the view of one with long standing in both the practice and the policy communities, he puts forth six propositions that will make sense to legislators and governors and, miracle of all, to teachers and parents, too.

Having a history—in this case, making sense out of a great deal of experience in education—will do much to help us create the schools that this society and its children need. Only an educator who has, practically, "seen-it-all" could have developed the powerful ideas that follow.

—Robert M. McClure
Series Editor
Director, Mastery In Learning Consortium,
NEA National Center for Innovation

Part One

Teacher Preparation

EDUCATION IN THE YEAR 2000

I'd like to focus on trends in the United States and around the world that I believe will have a profound impact on the nation's schools, and influence the way we educate our teachers.

THE DISADVANTAGED

I have no "crystal ball," of course. But it seems to me that one of the most dangerous and deeply depressing trends in our country today is the growing gap between the privileged and the poor, and the continued failure of our least advantaged students.

Everyone knows by now that by the year 2000 more than one-third of all children in the public schools will be Black or Hispanic and that these are precisely the children for whom the system has been least successful.

It's also true that in America today nearly one in four children under the age of six is officially classified as poor. They are nutritionally deprived, hugely disadvantaged, and many are drug depressed at birth. Without dramatic intervention, these children will come to school not only not ready to learn, but also with their potential dramatically diminished.

I'm convinced that all teacher education students, regardless of where they plan to teach, should learn about how the face of young America is changing. They should confront the hard facts of poverty in this country. They should understand that good education begins with good nutrition.

I'm suggesting that as we move toward the year 2000 the most urgent issue teachers will confront is this:

Will America continue to believe in opportunity for all? Or will we enter a new century spiritually impoverished, a deeply divided nation?

9

THE GLOBAL AGENDA

Albert Einstein wrote on one occasion[1] that everything has changed in the nuclear age except our "thinking," and I'm convinced that one of the most urgent challenges twenty-first century teachers will confront is educating all children to live with civility in a dangerous, interdependent world.

Today we live in a global village that is politically transformed, economically connected, and ecologically imperiled. It's a world where the ozone layer is depleted, our shorelines are polluted, and the tropical rain forests are being destroyed at the rate of 100,000 square kilometers every year. And yet for far too many of our students, their knowledge of our interdependent world goes about as far as the refrigerator door, the VCR knob, and the light switch on the wall.

During high school—and even college—students complete the required units. They are handed a diploma. What they fail to gain is a more coherent view of knowledge and a more authentic, more integrated view of life.

Over 50 years ago Mark Van Doren wrote that the connectedness of things is what the educator contemplates to the limit of one's capacity. And Van Doren concluded that the student who can begin—early in life—to see things as connected has begun the life of learning.[2] But how can this larger, more integrative view of life become a part of teacher preparation?

Frankly, by the year 2000, I'd like to see the core curriculum for teachers, especially elementary teachers, radically overhauled. I'd like to see a thematic approach to general education—one in which the disciplines are used to illuminate larger, more integrative ends.

As one approach, several years ago Art Levine and I suggested in our book, *A Quest for Common Learning*,[3] that the core curriculum might be organized not on the basis of the disciplines, but on the basis of what we called "the human commonalities," those universal human experiences that are found among all peoples and all cultures on the planet. Using those experiences that we share, those experiences that connect us to each other so that students within the curriculum would not only look at who they are but would understand how they're connected to other people, too.

First of all, we suggested that they should study and learn that everyone on the planet uses words to express feelings and ideas. And they might even learn a second language other than their own. In addition to the centrality of language, students might study such topics as our response to the aesthetic, our membership in groups and institutions, and our remarkable ability to recall the past and anticipate the future.

But at the heart of the new curriculum, I'd like to see a core course on birth, growth, and death. The sad truth is that most people on the planet live and die never reflecting on the mystery of their own existence—never really knowing about conception, never considering the sacredness of their own bodies, never discovering the essentiality of health, nor reflecting on the imperative of death.

Recently I brought my mother, who is 90, from a nursing home to live with us in her final years. She is in need of basic care. And every evening as we attend her I am reminded of the cycles of our existence. I'm also reminded of how in our modern age we have turned life's most basic functions over to institutions; how we no longer participate in birth; how children are cared for by what we call "providers"; how we are not called upon to care for loved ones at the end of their lives, and human bonding is diminished.

I am suggesting that all future teachers should begin by looking at life itself—at birth, at growth, and at death. Perhaps if we all know more about ourselves, we will respond more reverentially to the world around us.

TECHNOLOGY

This leads me to another trend that already has had major impact on teaching and learning.

Frankly, I find it remarkable that with all the talk about the crisis in our schools there has been virtually no mention of the technology revolution that quite literally has transformed our culture, and profoundly changed the lifestyles of our children.

Today's children watch television 4,000 hours before they even go to school; they know about computers; they're hooked on videocassettes; they're endlessly bombarded with rock music. Yet, day after day, these same children sit lethargically in classrooms, with only chalkboards, and perhaps an overhead projector. Teachers simply can't compete.

In a Carnegie Foundation survey of 22,000 teachers,[4] over half of the teachers wrote comments at the end. I was startled at the frequency with which they mentioned TV and technology. "Increasingly I feel 'obsolete,' like the rerun of an old movie," is the way one teacher put it. Another teacher said: "I feel I have to tap dance to keep their interest. It's frustrating to have to be ABC, CBS, NBC—and the Disney channel—when I really want to be PBS and NPR."

Teachers are not looking for excuses. There is clear evidence that TV is having a powerful and disturbingly negative impact on our children. After a 10-year study, researchers at Lund University in Sweden concluded that excessive TV viewing leads to antisocial behavior, emotional problems, poor learning, and violence.

I'm convinced that teachers for the next century should know about the impact technology is having on children. They

12

should be prepared to help them separate good messages from trash.

Is it too much to ask that by the next century every school would have a videotape library and a VCR in every classroom so teachers could use the New York Philharmonic, the Kennedy inauguration speech, a trip to the Louvre in Paris, and great moments in history and science to enrich their teaching? Frankly, it's a scandal that every other major enterprise in this country from airlines, to hospitals, to newspapers, to banking now uses technology to improve its work, while schools, of all places, are being damaged by the technology revolution.

CHILDREN AND FAMILIES

I'm beginning to suspect that in the United States today the family is a much more imperiled institution than the school, and, thus, that future teachers must be prepared to help troubled children.

In our survey of 22,000 teachers, 90 percent said that lack of parental support is a problem at their school, and 89 percent reported that abused and neglected children are a problem.[5] In their written comments teachers described in powerful and often poignant fashion their deep concern about the desperation of their children.

One teacher put her concern this way:

I'm sick and tired of seeing my bright-eyed first graders fade into "shadows of apathy" and become deeply troubled by age 10. These kids desperately need parents who deeply care.

Another teacher said:

The difficult part of teaching is not the academics. The difficult part is dealing with the great number of kids who

13

come from physically, socially, and financially stressed homes.

A veteran teacher from Minnesota wrote:

I worry about what's going on in neighborhoods and homes. More and more of my children seem neglected. Their lives are not well regulated. Meals, I know, are sporadic. They don't get enough sleep and it affects what they do in school. More than that, a lot of them seem anxious. I really worry about the future of these children.

An eighth grade history teacher in rural Maine told us:

My students face such enormous upheavals in their personal lives, I feel sometimes that I should just throw out the history book and help them deal with those deep hurts and worries that are more pressing on their minds.

A third grade teacher wrote:

We are raising a generation of emotionally stunted youth who will, in turn, raise a similar generation.

In 1988 we decided to go directly to the children. We surveyed 5,000 fifth and eighth graders and found that 40 percent go home every afternoon to an empty house.[6] Sixty percent said they wish they could spend more time with their mothers and their fathers. Two-thirds often wish they had more things to do, and 30 percent say their family never sits down together to eat a meal. Recently I talked with members of the school board in Rockford, Illinois, who said that an hour before school begins children huddle around the school door in the bitter cold because there's no one left at home.

Our daughter-in-law works in an inner-city Boston school. She tells how students hang around her desk after school not wanting to go home to an empty house or, even worse, not wanting to be abused. "The school," she said, "is the safest place they have."

I'm beginning to wonder if America really cares about its children.

I really do believe public education in this country is at a crossroads. Are the schools to be primarily educational institutions supported by the family or others? Or will schools in the next century become social service agencies, expected to meet not just the academic but the physical, social, and emotional needs of children, too? I suspect the answer lies somewhere in between.

By the twenty-first century, I'd like to see all big schools broken up into units of no more than 400 students each. I'd like to see every student assigned to a family-like unit of no more than 15 students to meet with a mentor at the beginning of each day to talk about their problems and know that someone truly cares.

THE SCHOOL CALENDAR AND THE CLOCK

My Grandfather Boyer was born in 1871. He lived 100 years. And during the century of his life the world moved from the horse-drawn plow to John Glenn's liftoff into space. When Grandpa was 96 I asked him about the schooling he'd had. He said he walked six miles each day and went several months—only in the winter—when he wasn't needed on the farm.

The point is that when our school calendar was set almost a century ago with nine months of study and three months off, over 90 percent of all schoolchildren were like Grandpa Boyer: living on the farm with their mothers and their fathers, working hard and coming home in the afternoon to help with chores, and taking summers off to tend the crops. In those days the school calendar mirrored the work and family patterns of the nation. But today less than 3 percent of America's families live on farms.

15

In most households, parents work away from home and about half the children now in first grade will live in one-parent families by the time they graduate from high school. Yet this country's children still go to school only about 175 days each year. This is out of phase with other countries and, most importantly perhaps, out of phase with family life. It's also out of phase with the exponential growth in what children should be learning.

Sometime by the year 2020, we should reorganize our schools into a year-round calendar with periodic breaks to give teachers time to get intellectually renewed. I firmly believe that such a restructuring would serve both the educational and the social needs of children.

I also believe that we must consider lengthening the school day, at least providing enrichment programs in the afternoon. As the latchkey problem grows, it seems to me we need afternoon enrichment programs in science, in computers, in music, and in athletics to keep children learning instead of sitting in an empty house or drifting in the streets.

CONCLUSION

Here, then, is my conclusion. Teachers for the next century

- must understand how America is changing and be prepared to help our least advantaged children;
- must have a perspective that is global and see things as connected;
- must help students cooperate rather than compete and find ways to use technology to help—not hurt—the learning process;
- must understand just how deeply children are in need. They must engage the parents and be not just competent, but deeply caring, too.

As John Gardner observed, a nation is never finished.[7] You can't build it and leave it standing as the pharaohs did the pyramids. It has to be recreated for each new generation. I'm convinced that the most urgent task our nation now confronts is reaffirming schools and building a better future for our children.

NOTES

[1]Lapp, Ralph E., "The Einstein Letter That Started It All," *New York Times Magazine,* August 2, 1964.

[2]Van Doren, M., *Liberal Education* (New York: Henry Holt, 1943), 115.

[3]Boyer, Ernest L., and Levine, Arthur, *A Quest for Common Learning,* Carnegie Foundation for the Advancement of Teaching (Princeton, N.J.: Princeton University Press, 1981).

[4]*The Condition of Teaching: A State-by-State Analysis* (Princeton, N.J.: Carnegie Foundation for the Advancement of Teaching, 1990).

[5]Ibid.

[6]*The Carnegie Foundation for the Advancement of Teaching Student Survey* (Princeton, N.J.: Carnegie Foundation for the Advancement of Teaching, 1988).

[7]Gardner, John W., *Excellence: Can We Be Equal and Excellent Too?* rev. ed. (New York: Norton, 1984), 162.

Part Two

Early Childhood Education

PROGRAMS FOR OUR YOUNGEST CHILDREN

I'm increasingly convinced that if the school movement is to succeed, we must give top priority to the early years of education. This is the time that's absolutely crucial. If little children do not have a good beginning, if in the early years a solid educational foundation is not laid, it will be almost impossible to compensate fully for the failure later on.

Almost everyone, at least in theory, agrees with this conviction, from the president on down. But I must tell you that it is still largely theory and that what we urgently need is a plan of action to get us from where we are to where we must be going.

NUTRITION

How should we proceed? First, I believe the evidence is overwhelming that if little children are to succeed educationally, they must have good nutrition. And yet the harsh truth is that because of growing poverty in this country many children are physically and emotionally at risk even before they're born. The infant death rate in Washington, D.C., in Baltimore, Maryland, and in Detroit, Michigan, is higher than in Jamaica. Consider also that a boy who is born in Harlem today has a lower life expectancy than a boy who is born in Bangladesh.

It's also true that in the United States today, the richest nation in the world, nearly one of every four children under the age of six is officially classified as poor. They're undernourished, hugely disadvantaged. If we continue to neglect the crisis of poor children in this country, the future of the nation is imperiled both educationally and culturally.

21

A recent report of the Harvard School of Public Health[1] revealed that a child who is not well fed will have a lower IQ, have a shorter attention span, and get lower grades in school. The harsh truth is that the federal nutrition program that provides food for poor mothers and their babies is still shockingly underfunded.

Winston Churchill, who had a way with words, said on one occasion that there is no finer investment in any community than putting milk into little babies. I'm convinced that good education in this country begins with good nutrition.

LINGUISTICS

Between now and the year 2000 we must have universal preschool programs for every disadvantaged child, to help him or her overcome not just poor nutrition, but linguistic deprivation, too. The truth is that far too many children grow up in environments where they do not hear sentences well spoken. There is no syntax. They hear only blunt commands, shouts, and their questions go unanswered. So, just as little children are denied good nutrition, other children do not get the linguistic environment they need to begin to build the vocabulary that prepares them for future schooling.

I found it enormously significant that in a recent national survey of the National Association of Elementary School Principals,[2] two-thirds of the elementary school principals surveyed said that preschool education is very important in determining the academic success of children later on; an additional 12 percent said that it is certainly somewhat important. This means that three-fourths of today's administrators believe that preschool education is important.

We know it works. Frankly, I consider it a national disgrace that 20 years after the Head Start program was authorized by Congress to help disadvantaged three- and four-year-olds, only about 30 percent of the eligible children are being served. President Bush in his State of the Union message declared this as the first goal: By the year 2000 every child in this country should come to school ready to learn. He has also announced that this goal will be met. But it is my conviction that if this objective is to be accomplished, we need full funding of the child nutrition program at the federal level. We need full funding of Head Start at the federal level to overcome the shocking gap between the privileged and the disadvantaged. It will not happen just by saying that it will.

Is it too much to hope that while this nation is spending millions to send rockets into orbit it will also be willing to help save the lives of little children here on earth?

THE BASIC SCHOOL

There's a third step that we might take to strengthen early education. We should reorganize the first years of formal schooling into a single unit called the Basic School.

The Basic School, as I see it, would be nongraded. It would combine kindergarten through grade four. It would give top priority to language. Children from the very first day would be reading and writing, telling stories, and talking about words in a climate the foreign language people like to call the saturation method.

It's my belief that children come to school hugely ready for the empowerment of language. They have already mastered the syntax. Any child who can speak and listen, in my judgment, is absolutely ready to read and write.

Lewis Thomas wrote that childhood is for language.[3] It's in the early years that curiosity abounds. This is the time when children are empowered in the use of words, and when their use of symbols exponentially increases.

I'm suggesting that the top priority of the early years must be to help all children become proficient in the written and the spoken word. Language isn't just another subject. It's the means by which all the subjects are pursued. It's not just another skill. It's the means by which we reach out and are connected to each other. And there's no more shattering discovery for parents than to discover they have a child who cannot adequately communicate and connect through the miracle of language.

If, in the first years, we could help our children master joyfully the use of symbols so they could speak and listen and write and understand the language that would allow them to become socially and intellectually empowered, that would be the most sacred act that we could extend them. If we could accomplish that, they would be positioned, in my opinion, to live with confidence later on. That should be, it seems to me, the Basic School's most important goal.

CLASS SIZE

I also believe strongly that there should be no classes in the Basic School of more than 15 students each. Frankly, I think it's silly to suggest class size doesn't matter—especially in the early years when children are developing intellectually and emotionally and urgently need one-on-one attention.

Occasionally I take three or four of my grandchildren to a fast-food restaurant, and I come back a basket case. The very fact that there's no ketchup on the floor and they're still alive gives me a huge cause for inner rejoicing and satisfaction. Now, I love these children very much, but imagine me dealing with not just keeping ketchup off the floor, but helping little minds develop individually. That awesome obligation cannot be fulfilled when there are 20 or 30 children in a room—at least not as successfully as when one adult is working more intimately with them.

In Japan the teacher ratio is 40 to 1. But I have a grandchild who has been at a Japanese school. That's where they treat teaching as rote learning. It's the cookie-cutter model, with each child moving along the assembly line. "Pick up your pencils. Put them down." But that's not the American way of learning—we are interested in each individual child.

The Basic School then, in my judgment, requires an intimate climate for learning. While I give emphasis to language, let me underscore the point that social and emotional development for little children is absolutely crucial, too. This means that we need small classes to overcome the anonymity of bigness, to help little children feel connected not only to each other but to a teacher who understands them, both in their heads and in their hearts.

Several years ago the state of Indiana compared the achievements of first graders in large classes with those in classes of less than 10 students each. The evidence was overwhelming that children in the small classes did much better. Big surprise! Yet today, far too many first grade classes in this country have over 20 students each; while at the other end of the academic ladder, when students are finishing their doctoral degrees, they are working with a mentor, one-to-one.

What we are doing in this country is giving the most help to those who need it least.

I'm talking about reordering the educational priorities of this country by focusing on the first years of formal education, by having the smallest classes in grades one through four. I'm convinced that if this nation would give as much status to first grade teachers as we give to full professors, that one act alone could revitalize the nation's schools.

25

CURRICULUM

But what about the curriculum in the Basic School? Now I'll stop preaching and start to meddle. What should all elementary students learn?

Beyond language and computation I'd like to see a course of study in the Basic School that focuses not on separate academic subjects, such as history and civics and geography, but rather on the integration of ideas toward some larger understanding, so that all students could obtain a more coherent view of knowledge and a more integrated, more authentic view of life.

What intrigues me is that young children are naturally integrators in the way they think. They're always searching for connections. Little children are dissatisfied with snippets of information. That's why they keep asking "Why?" It's only when we go up the academic ladder (or is it down the academic chute?) that we are willing to be content with trivial information; we are willing to sit still for something called a Carnegie Unit, which takes information out of context and gives it to us in small isolated slices. Young children are not content with fragmentation of the world that they see around them.

Children should learn how people on the planet respond to the aesthetic, how they express themselves through music, theater, and the visual arts. All children should learn how all members of the planet engage themselves in groups and in institutions. This is an experience shared by all cultures. Children should study how we are all part of nature and learn about the science and ecology of our planet in which, as Lewis Thomas said, we are all embedded as working parts.[4] All children in the Basic School should learn how we can recall the past and anticipate the future. As far as I know, we are the only species on the planet with a capacity to put ourselves in time and space.

26

Finally, at the heart of this human commonalities curriculum, I believe all students should study the most fundamental experience that we all share, the miracle of birth, growth, and death. The sad truth is that most people on the planet are born and live and die without ever reflecting on the mystery of life. They never understand the miracle of conception. They never learn about the essentialism of health. They often know more about the carburetors of their cars than about the inner organs of their bodies. They never consider the imperative of death until suddenly their own mortality is threatened.

I am suggesting that the six human commonality themes I have just discussed—language, the arts, our heritage, nature, historical perspective, and life itself—form the core of our existence. They connect us to each other. They also provide, I believe, a useful framework by which the Basic School curriculum might integratively be shaped.

If children learned more about who they are and where they fit, they would, in later life, be able to respond more reverentially to the world around them. So let's not get them trapped in the little boxes we call academic departments. These boxes may serve the needs of universities; they don't serve children very well. Let's use the subjects as integrators to help young people understand who they are, and how they relate to other human beings.

ASSESSMENT AND EVALUATION

This brings me to the crucial issue of assessment in the Basic School. How do we evaluate the students? I do believe we need to assess the performance of our students in language and computation at the completion of grade four. It would also be my urgent hope that no child would leave that grade without feeling empowered in the use of symbols.

In order to assure that a solid foundation has been laid, and that the tools of learning have been mastered, it seems to me that before fourth grade we should trust the teacher, who is able to evaluate each student intuitively and to see all the talents. We should not try to reduce evaluation to a number, or to put checkmarks on a paper. I believe that very often we measure that which matters least. Through standardized evaluation we too frequently screen out talent rather than release it. We tell children at a very early age that they're failures before they ever discover who they are, or what they might become.

The truth is, of course, that questions that are judged to be critical of the student, even benign questions, can stifle the creativity of children. I know a story that whimsically illustrates the point. A minister, who was giving a sermon one Sunday morning, was telling the children about a boy who was sitting under a tree in the woods. "And," he said, "as the boy was sitting there, a furry little creature with a long tail came running by and scampered up a tree." Then, to try to engage them, the minister asked the children, "What do you think the little creature was?" One bright-eyed fellow in the front row raised his hand and said, "Minister, it sure sounds like a squirrel to me. But I guess you want me to say it was Baby Jesus."

Obviously, the trick here was to figure out what the preacher wanted, not just the answer that seemed obvious to the boy.

About 30 years ago, my wife and I were called to school. We were told that one of our children hadn't tested very well, and that he wouldn't do well in school. We knew better. They called him special. We called him special for quite a different reason. But the label stuck, and he was quite lackadaisical during his school experience.

One teacher described him as very dreamy, and the "dreaminess" came out later on. For the last 10 years, let the record show, this son has been living in a Mayan village, the only non-Mayan who has lived there in a thousand years. He's been supervising six Mayan schools. He's learned a new language. He's been building bridges across chasms that even the British engineers couldn't manage. He's been understanding a culture profoundly different from his own, but one that has the same commonalities I just described.

I've been reflecting on the gap between the tests and real life. A year or so ago, it occurred to me what the problem was: that the schools just didn't give him the right tests. I mean, they just didn't ask him, "How do you live in a Mayan village?" And they didn't ask him how to build a bridge. They didn't ask him how to cope with another culture. They didn't ask him, "How do you intuitively survive?" They asked him to put little checkmarks on a piece of paper. They didn't tap what he knew or the talents that were stored up. These were ignored by the rigid screening that caused the psychometrician to say he was nongifted.

What a tragic miscalculation to kill the human spirit! What we're doing too often through testing is encouraging conformity and competition, when in fact the world urgently needs creativity and cooperation. Howard Gardner, in his provocative book *Frames of Mind,*[5] reminds us that children have not only verbal intelligence, but also logical intelligence, spatial intelligence, artistic intelligence, and intuitive and social intelligence. These intelligences must be encouraged, not neglected.

James Agee and Walker Evans once wrote that with every child who is born—no matter what the circumstance—the potentiality of the human race is born again.[6] This should be the vision for the early years of all children as we look to the year 2000 and beyond.

INTERGENERATIONAL CONNECTIONS

I'm increasingly disturbed by the intergenerational separations in our culture. Margaret Mead noted that a healthy society is one in which three generations vitally interact with one another.[7] But what we seem to be creating in America today is a horizontal culture in which babies are in nurseries, three-year-olds are in day care centers, children are in schools, and adults are in the workplace. Retirees are in villages or living all alone. The intergenerational connectedness has been snapped, and I think we're not communicating with those of different ages. There is something unhealthy about living from birth to death and talking only with one's peers.

The challenge of the next decade is to build intergenerational institutions, such as having grandparents tutor children in the schools, having high school children engage in community service and work in day care centers with little children.

My parents lived for several years in a retirement village that had a day care center. Every morning about 50 four- and five-year-olds would come trucking out, and every grandparent had an adopted grandchild. When I called my father, he wouldn't complain about his aches and pains. He'd tell me about his "little friend," as he called him. When I'd visit him, I'd see the wonderful drawings scotchtaped on the wall, as any grandparent is inclined to do. There seemed to be something authentic about the interrelationship between the little child who was inspired by the agony and the courage of someone who was growing older and an 80-year-old who was stimulated by the energy and the innocence of youth. That to me is the chemistry that makes a culture work. Incidentally, I heard recently that the reason grandparents and grandchildren get along so well is that they have a common enemy.

What I am suggesting is this: While we need to focus on our schools, they can't do the job alone. We must start looking not only at the condition of education, but most especially at the condition of families and the condition of our children. Perhaps, then, in the next century, we will have not just school boards in our communities, we may also have children's boards . . . some way in which we can look at the services that are needed overall.

We are at a crossroads. I've concluded that the ideal Basic School would have a social service unit with a nurse and a counselor, and perhaps a social worker, especially when serving needy children, to give backup help to teachers. But we cannot have an island of excellence in a sea of indifference; parents simply must become more actively involved in the education of their children. This means turning off television from time to time. It means reading aloud to children. It means asking about homework. It also means making regular school visits.

I'm convinced that in the next century, if not before, employers should give parents a day off with pay—several times a year—so that they can go to school for teachers' conferences and spend time with their children in the classroom. Better schooling must become everybody's business.

CONCLUSION

Here, then, is my conclusion. The 1990s must become the decade for early education, since this is where the crusade for better schooling will be won or lost. I propose as national objectives that we have good nutrition for every child; that we have universal preschool education for every disadvantaged child; that we have an ungraded Basic School with small classes, with a focus on language, with a curriculum with coherence, with a restructured calendar, and with a deeply caring climate. Above all, I propose that parents become active partners in the process.

31

I know these are audacious goals. I'm convinced that the most urgent task our generation now confronts is renewing our commitment to the early years of learning and to educating all children to their full potential.

NOTES

[1] From Physician Task Force on Hunger in America, *Hunger in America: The Growing Epidemic* (Middletown, Conn.: Wesleyan University Press, 1985), 101.

[2] *The Basic School Concept,* National Association of Elementary School Principals Opinion Survey of Elementary School Principals (Washington, D.C.: National Association of Elementary School Principals, April 1990).

[3] Thomas, Lewis. *Late Night Thoughts Listening to Mahler* (New York: Viking, 1983), 52.

[4] Thomas, L., *The Medusa and the Snail: More Notes of a Biology Watcher* (New York: Viking, 1979), 174.

[5] Gardner, H., *Frames of Mind: The Theory of Multiple Intelligences* (New York: Basic Books, 1983).

[6] Agee, J., and Evans, Walker, *Let Us Now Praise Famous Men* (Boston: Houghton Mifflin; Cambridge: Riverside Press, 1941).

[7] Mead, Margaret, *Culture and Commitment: A Study of the Generation Gap* (Garden City, N.Y.: Natural History Press, 1970), 2.

Part Three

A National Education Index

A FRAMEWORK FOR STATE ACCOUNTABILITY

The 1990 Fortune Education Summit focused on the states' role in providing a report card on the nation's schools. It's a topic that couldn't be more timely. In a PBS documentary, "The Civil War," historian Shelby Foote observed that, before the war, Americans said, "The United States *are*." After the war we said, "The United States *is*." We came to think of ourselves, he said, as *one* people.

I'm convinced that something similar to this is happening to us in education. For most of our history, responsibility for schooling in this country was largely local. Schools were *locally* controlled, paid for by *local* taxes, and student progress was measured by each teacher—and reported personally to parents.

But now, something quite remarkable is going on. Today, the citizens of this country are increasingly dissatisfied with a piecemeal approach to education. For the first time in our history, Americans appear to be more concerned about *national* outcomes than about *local* school control. And they're demanding evidence that our huge, $180 billion annual investment in public education is paying off.

One could argue, of course, that a *national* view of education goes back to Thomas Jefferson who eloquently argued that education *and* democracy are inextricably interlocked. And surely it could be argued that Horace Mann had a *national* view of education when he zealously promoted the common school for the common good.

But the essential point is that, while the *ends* of public education were national in scope, the *means* were local and, for years, we've believed that each school—acting largely on its own—could serve effectively the civic and economic interests of the nation. But, today, all signals suggest that we're more than ready for a national policy in education.

- Consider, for example, that during the 1988 presidential campaign, Mr. Bush defined himself as the "Education President."
- Consider, also, that in 1989 the president called together the governors from all 50 states for the nation's first education summit.
- Consider, further, that President Bush, in his first State of the Union message, announced six national education goals that, shortly thereafter, were adopted by the governors from all 50 states.
- And consider, especially, that—according to a fall 1989 Gallup Poll[1]—more than 60 percent of Americans surveyed now say they favor *national* standards, a *national* curriculum, and *national* tests for students.

The message—it seems to me—is absolutely clear. After years of vigorously defending local school control, the nation is now supporting—indeed almost demanding—national leadership in education, while still maintaining vitality at the local level. It's a new challenge, something we've never faced before, and how we respond surely will shape public education and the nation for years to come.

Former Governor Garrey Carruthers of New Mexico captured the spirit of the times precisely when he said, "People will look back at the period between 1989 and 1991 and say it was the most dynamic ever in the history of public education."

A NATIONAL EDUCATION INDEX

How, then, should we proceed?

I'm convinced it's time to go beyond goals—important as they are—and begin to talk more precisely about education

36

standards and how progress toward national objectives can be measured. Specifically, I'd like to suggest the creation of a National Education Index that could serve as a framework of accountability for the states.

A National Education Index could operate much like our current economic index—warning us when we are off course, and providing reassurance when we're moving in the right direction. A National Index could guide the states in their push for school reform, while also making it possible to measure progress nationwide. And with such an index, states would learn from one another. Above all, a National Index could, for the first time, provide agreed-upon standards to assess education progress.

What, then, might be included in a National Education Index?

Student Achievement

The first and most obvious standard relates to the school completion rates of students. If the dropout rate is to be dramatically reduced, as the president has proposed, the National Education Index should report annually on the percentage of students in every state who complete successfully their prescribed course of study.

But the most essential element of a national report card relates not just to persistence, but to learning. This *is* the bottom line. And, in shaping a National Education Index, every state should respond to these essential questions:

- What are the English and mathematics proficiencies of each student? After all, these are the basic tools of learning.
- How do students perform on general knowledge tests that evaluate their knowledge in key academic subjects?
- Does the state give priority to writing? And is a senior paper a requirement for high school graduation?

Let me quickly add that, while I strongly support national assessment, I'm also concerned that student evaluation be linked directly to school goals, and that we measure not just the recall of isolated facts, but that we develop ways to measure other essential skills, like creativity and independent thinking.

- California, for example, has developed new tests that are *performance* oriented—procedures that ask students to write, to solve problems, and to prepare scientific reports on their own.
- Vermont has begun a pioneering assessment program in all fourth and eighth grade mathematics and writing classes that includes portfolios of student work. Assessments for other subjects such as history, science, and citizenship are being developed.
- Students in Connecticut are being measured on a series of independent projects that may take them a semester to complete.

In the end, what we test is what we teach, and there's an urgent need to evaluate not just the verbal intelligence of students, but their aesthetic, spatial, and intuitive intelligence as well.

I'm suggesting that our first and most essential task is to clarify school goals and *then* find effective ways to evaluate the performance of each student.

Perhaps, in this connection, it's time to convene a blue-ribbon panel of gifted scholars and teachers to suggest an appropriate curriculum for Century 21—using models from leading states—and also to suggest ways by which student progress can be most effectively assessed.

The Condition of Teaching

This leads to priority number two. After all is said and done, the quality of our schools can be no greater than the dignity we assign to teaching. And a National Education Index surely should ask governors to respond to these essential questions:

- First, does your state have a plan for attracting outstanding students into teaching? And does your state provide mentoring?
- Also, what special strategies do you have to attract teachers in mathematics and science, so the president's objective can be achieved?
- Further, does your state have a mandated in-service education program? Are sabbaticals, fellowships, and teacher institutes provided?
- Finally, what are the starting and maximum salaries of teachers? And how do the salaries in your state compare with others in the region?

For several years, we at the Carnegie Foundation have surveyed teachers, asking them to report on working conditions in their state. Our 1990 survey[2] revealed dramatic differences from one place to another, with many teachers feeling more responsible, but less empowered.

- Teachers in Mississippi and South Carolina, for example, gave generally favorable ratings to reform efforts in their states, while those in many other states were less encouraged.
- South Carolina also has a "Teacher Cadet" program that encourages bright high school students to enter the profession.
- North Carolina has a "Teacher Fellows" program to

encourage students in the top 10 percent of their high school class to go into the profession.

- And West Virginia now requires new teachers to complete successfully a one-year teacher internship—working closely with a mentor.

I'm suggesting that it's simply impossible to achieve national education goals without focusing on teachers. And, in developing a National Education Index, all states must be held accountable for teacher recruitment and renewal.

School Climate

This brings me to a third essential theme. I'm convinced that a National Education Index also must focus on "school climate," and begin by asking states to report on the quality of facilities—buildings, classrooms, laboratories, and the like.

This may sound pretty basic, but a recent report by the Education Writers of America[3] found that the majority of our schools are in disturbingly poor condition and that the worst ones have leaking roofs, clogged toilets, and bunsen burners that won't work. Does a state really deserve a passing grade if it sends its children—year in and year out—to shockingly shabby, ill-equipped buildings that are in such contrast to shopping malls, gleaming office buildings, and glitzy new hotels?

School climate also involves class size. According to the 1989 Gallup Poll,[4] 82 percent of the school parents surveyed believe classes should be smaller, and a large percentage said they would be willing to pay higher taxes if class size could be reduced.

Further, during our study of the American high school,[5] I became convinced that we have not just a school problem, but a youth problem in this country; too many students feel unconnected to the larger world. We found an anonymity in many large urban schools; it seemed quite obvious to me that many students drop out of school simply because no one noticed that they had, in fact, dropped in.

I believe that, in preparing a National Education Index, every state should be asked: In your state, what is the average class size, especially in the early years when students need one-on-one attention?

- The state of Tennessee conducted a statewide study of the effects of class size in kindergarten to grade three and found that students in small classes made greater academic gains.
- Several years ago, Texas mandated a 1 to 22 maximum teacher-student ratio in kindergarten through grade three. Here, again, it's reported that student achievement has improved.
- Finally, the Indiana General Assembly legislated a program called "Project Prime Time" to reduce class size in kindergarten and first grade.

I'm suggesting that a National Education Index must focus on school climate, considering not just the physical facilities, but other important matters—such as class size.

School Finance

Fourth, a National Education Index also must look at the financing of public education, and ask if schools are adequately supported.

In this connection, our 1990 teacher survey[6] revealed that, during one five-month period, teachers themselves spent—on average—$250 of their own money to pay for materials and supplies. If we extend this across the year and include all teachers, that would total over a billion dollars!

It's obvious, of course, that money alone is not the answer. But it's equally obvious that we can't have education on the cheap. And, in a National Education Index, it seems appropriate to ask: What is the per-pupil expenditure in every state?

Perhaps it's not quite fair to rank order all the states in their per student expenditure—since regional costs *are* very different. So, maybe the question really is: How does your state compare *regionally*, taking local cost-of-living matters into consideration?

Regarding financing, there is also the absolutely crucial matter of equity, an issue that is being debated all across the country. Over the last couple of years, courts in New Jersey, Texas, and Kentucky have ruled that wide discrepancies in school finance cannot be defended. In Kentucky, for example, per pupil expenditures had ranged from $1,800 to $4,200 per district. In other states the disparities are even wider.

We may disagree about the *absolute* point at which an effective education can be delivered, but surely wide gaps are unacceptable—especially when the least support often goes to children who are least advantaged. And I'm convinced a state should get a low mark on an Education Index if gross inequities in funding are permitted.

Incidentally, states should not just assume that its citizens won't pay for improving education. A CBS News/ *New York Times* poll[7] found that people say they *are* willing to pay higher taxes to help schools. But the key, I'm convinced, is making it clear precisely how the money will be used and how high taxes can assure higher performance of the students.

Accountability and Intervention

Fifth, a National Education Index also should examine the procedures by which the schools are governed. The era of burgeoning bureaucracy is over, and states must untangle the web of regulations that have strangled schools. After defining standards, states must give a great deal of freedom to the local schools and hold them responsible for ends, not means.

The California Department of Education has introduced a statewide plan of assessment in secondary schools. And the National Governors Association is using school restructuring and more accountability to assure that there will be quality schools for all students—a move that should be included in any National Education Index.

Consider, for example, these essential questions:

- Does the state have clearly defined goals?
- Is an assessment procedure in place that requires schools to report annually on their progress?
- Are local schools held accountable for *outcomes,* not *procedures?*
- And does the state have clearly defined methods of intervention in case a school is failing?

Regarding intervention, a range of options should be considered.

- For example, a state might put a school on probation, asking for continuing assessment.
- Or a state might assign a senior adviser to the school who would spend time working with teachers, counselors, and administrators.
- The state also might conclude that the school has a fiscal crisis and provide emergency assistance—proposing how additional resources should be spent.
- It's also possible that poor leadership is the problem, and the state would remove the principal or superintendent.

- And, finally, the state might remove the local school board—as New Jersey has done in the past—or even close a school—a strategy of last resort.
- In recent years, eight other states—Arkansas, Georgia, Illinois, Kentucky, New Mexico, Ohio, South Carolina, and Texas—have proposed or enacted legislation dealing with "academic bankruptcy" or "failed" districts. The intervention methods in these plans involve restructuring the districts, withholding funds, or firing the superintendent.

Again, local school control is crucial, but it's insufficient. In the end, students must be served, and if a school, for whatever reason, does not provide an effective education, state officials have both a legal and a moral obligation to intervene.

Building Partnerships

The sixth and last part of a National Education Index would focus on school partnerships.

In the past, parents were often deeply supportive of the schools. But in recent years this connection has been strained—or even broken—with the changes in lifestyles.

President Bush's first, and I believe most essential, goal is that—by the year 2000—all children will come to school ready to learn. But for this to be accomplished, we urgently must rebuild the bridges between families and schools, especially in the early years when the foundation for learning will be laid.

- The state of Florida has a program that awards certificates to what are called "Red Carpet Schools"—institutions that welcome parents, open school facilities to families, and involve parents directly in the education of their children.

In addition to parent participation, linkages with the workplace are crucial, too. According to a recent Roper Poll,[8] 72 percent of businesses surveyed supported giving employees time off to teach in the school systems. Edward Donley, at the U.S. Chamber of Commerce, said, "the American public considers the business community the education safety net for the nation." And it's enormously encouraging that more than 70 percent of all schools now have some sort of partnership with business.

But I believe it's not just the projects, it's the *power* of the opinion that matters most. When business leaders talk, lawmakers listen. And the fact that *Fortune Magazine* just held its fourth annual summit meeting on education sends a powerfully constructive signal to the nation.

I'm suggesting that schools cannot do the job alone. A National Education Index should ask every state to respond to key questions such as these:

- Are statewide programs in place that involve parents more actively in the education of their children?
- How is the support of the business community promoted in your state?

Public education is everybody's business. Partnerships that link the school, the workplace, and the home must be sustained and strengthened.

NATIONAL COUNCIL

This brings me to one final issue. Who, in fact, should be in charge of the national evaluation of school performance? Where should the responsibility be placed?

It seems clear to me we need a new kind of structure to guide the move toward national accountability in education.

Several years ago, at the Business Roundtable, we proposed a National Council on Educational Standards—comprised of distinguished citizens—to keep the president, the Congress, and the public well informed.

Recently, the Senate voted to establish a national panel to monitor education progress. This action followed on the heels of a House bill that would form a similar oversight commission. Meanwhile, the governors—in cooperation with the White House—moved to form their own 14-member panel of governors, federal officials, and congressional representatives to track state progress.

These different strategies must be sorted out; it's still unclear who will ultimately be responsible for monitoring education progress. But I remain convinced that we urgently need a new, well-regarded education panel, one that has both autonomy and integrity, and that can speak with authority and political independence, too.

The new council—whatever its form—should, of course, embrace the president's six goals. But, to implement these goals, the council also needs a framework—with specific standards—by which it can measure state-by-state progress. And I've suggested that a National Education Index be established and include a report card on

- the academic achievement of the student
- the condition of teachers
- school climate
- school finance
- state governance assessments
- and the partnership strategies in each state.

An index that focuses on these essential matters would make it possible for us to have national goals, statewide accountability, and creative leadership at the local level—a combination that is crucial if we are to create a truly excellent public system of education in the nation.

NOTES

[1] Elam, Stanley M., and Gallup, Alec M., "The 21st Annual Gallup Poll on the Public's Attitudes Toward the Public Schools," *Phi Delta Kappan,* September 1989, 41–54.

[2] *The Condition of Teaching: A State-by-State Analysis* (Princeton, N.J.: Carnegie Foundation for the Advancement of Teaching, 1990).

[3] *Wolves at the Schoolhouse Door: An Investigation of the Condition of Public School Buildings* (Washington, D.C.: Education Writers of America, 1989).

[4] Elam and Gallup, "The 21st Annual Gallup Poll."

[5] Boyer, Ernest L., *High School: A Report on Secondary Education in America,* (Hagerstown, Md.: Harper-Collins Publishers, 1983).

[6] *The Condition of Teaching.*

[7] CBS News/*New York Times* Poll. Interviewing done October 26–31, 1990.

[8] *Roper Reports,* 90–8, August 1990.